There is no PTSD

By Karl Smith

"Forces beyond your control can take away everything you possess except one thing, your freedom to choose how you will respond to the situation."

Viktor E. Frankl (1905-1997)

ISBN-13: 978-0-9954599-6-0

Published by Ann Jaloba Publishing

The moral right of Karl Smith to be identified as the author has been asserted in accordance with the copyright design and patents act 1988

Note to Readers

DEDICATION

There are so many, genuinely. Steve Miller from Weight Loss Master for the inspiration in the first place and guidance, all the contributors in this book for their work and support, amazing mentors, therapists and coaches in your own profession.

Mark Williams and the Police Firearms Officers Association for the belief and the support when I first started out on my journey in changework and for letting me be part of such an amazing and unique organisation.

Dov Baron, my mentor and Inspiration for getting me to realise . . . I'm the ONLY . . .

My family. All of them for being there for me, thick and thin and for just being you... Thank you.

To those who have fallen in service and paid the ultimate price for protecting us, and to those great men and women worldwide who still protect and look after us 24/7 while we get on with our daily lives, Thank you.

Ubique Quo Fas Et Gloria Ducunt
"Everywhere That Right And Glory Lead"

Remember, It's not the Critic that counts

No D in PTSD

Contents

Contents

FOREWORD

By Lt Col (Retd) Richard Dorney MBE, MSc

When Karl asked me to write the foreword for this book I was somewhat surprised. I am neither an academic nor a clinician and I don't do therapy! I am however no stranger to trauma; I spent almost 40 years in the Queen's uniform 'discouraging' her enemies in various places that don't appear in the travel agent's brochures.

I saw trauma and I have been responsible for the management of those suffering the consequences of it. I set up the Army Trauma Risk Management Training Team and I have spent many years teaching people both in and out of uniform how to recognise and manage people who may be suffering poor mental health with the aim of facilitating early intervention.

Karl's personal story is one of inspiration and optimism. He found a way out of the darkness and now helps many to find their own path. Whilst PTSD is far from the commonest mental health disorder (affecting about 5% in the UK population), it can be debilitating. Even in the uniformed services it is not the most common presentation (overtaken by anxiety, depression and substance misuse among others) but the risks from frequent or continual exposure are very significant in these groups.

I was confused by the title of the book; 'No 'D' in PTSD'; this condition most certainly is a disorder because it affects the ability of sufferers to function and to live fulfilling lives. After some thought, I realised that the message in the title is simply one of hope. PTSD like most mental health disorders is treatable and recovery rates are good, so the 'D' in most cases can with time and help, be removed. The treatments of choice by clinicians are CBT and EMDR, both of which are fully explained in the pages of this book. These treatments are recommended in the UK by the National Institute for Health and Clinical Excellence (NICE) because they have been subjected to large randomised control trials and have excellent evidence bases. There are of course other therapies available and this book will guide you through the confusing terminology and how the treatments work. Each section is written by an expert in a particular field.

PTSD remains a controversial diagnosis and there is much disagreement about what constitutes a traumatic event and the thresholds for diagnosis as a disorder. There are also disagreements about the effectiveness of various treatments. The problem with treatment and or therapy for mental health problems is that our mental health is complex and unique to us; none of us will present in the same way when we become unwell. There is no doubt that the therapies mentioned in these pages have helped many, sometimes when other treatments have not been effective. Symptoms can be treated and it will be interesting to see how the research develops around hypnosis. Hypnotherapy can have powerful results for many people; the trick is to take medical advice and to find the therapy and the therapist that works for you.

Karl and his colleagues will guide you through how some of these treatments work, from Karl's unique Kinetic Shift techniques to Psy tap, CBT and EMDR. If you are worried about what happens and how it works, this book will give you a unique insight into the various treatment methods.

The message though is clear, there are many effective treatments out there, recovery can and will happen in most cases but it can take time and effort so, there is always help and light at the end of the tunnel, but you need to ask for it. Symptoms are often made worse by delayed presentation, denial and substance misuse.

It takes courage to ask for help, especially for those who have served in the uniforms of their nation. By getting help you can banish the D in the disorder and learn to cope with life's challenges. If this book encourages debate and discussion it will be a positive; talking about mental health is vital and will help to banish the stigma which for so many is an obstacle to help seeking. If someone close to you is suffering, get them to read this book. Karl got himself out of the hole and with help, patience and encouragement so can you.

Lt Col (Retd) Richard Dorney MBE, MSc

Director Strongmind Resiliency Training Ltd

www.strongmindresilience.co.uk

No D in PTSD

HOW TO USE THIS BOOK

This is a practical guide and I hope a convincer. By that I mean a convincer that you do not need to be burdened with this problem any more. I have tried to make it as accessible and easy to use as I can, so here is a quick guide to steer you through.

This is how it works. Firstly there is a bit about yours truly. This isn't there to feed my ego but to show you that it is possible to overcome what has been thrown at you and get on to have a great life.

Section Two tells stories from the frontline. Soldiers, police, and health workers say what happened to them, what help was out there and how they coped. These people have been through the tough times and have inspired me.

Then some of my esteemed colleagues write about the ways they help people suffering from trauma. We are lucky that we now live in a world where there are quite a few new therapies which are proven to help. I hope you will enjoy hearing from some of the best people in the business about their particular therapy, how it works, and who it suits. And I have written about a particular way of doing things which I have developed called Kinetic Shift. This should give you a good start in choosing what you think would help you.

I hope that this will give you some information about what is out there to help you. I have given contact details for them so if you think they have what will work for you then get in contact with them.

In their own words, they talk about how they have learned that paying attention to how the mind works is not something for old hippies or cardigan-wearing therapists but a down-to-earth way of coping with stressful or even traumatic events.

They know that often in our workplaces it is seen as soft or daft to talk about how we feel, so they tell you how you can start to do it. We know that often the support from the top brass is missing on this, but that doesn't need to stop us.

I hope that all gets you going on a new and better path. And remember you are not alone.

Karl Smith

Section 1

In this section , I tell you a bit more about myself and how I ended up helping others with PTSD. I also give you my views about how being in uniform affects our behaviours and personality. Finally, I take a look at the history of stress disorders and combat, and show that it is nothing new.

No D in PTSD

INTRODUCTION: A CAR, A HOUSE AND A TRAUMA. . . HOW I GOT HERE

So it starts with me placing my kit away in the police station, for some strange reason my locker always looked like a grenade had gone off in it, it was a mess. Now I had served 12 years in the British Army before joining the Police, so you would have thought I knew better. But the state of my locker was about to become the least of my problems.

The date was August 4th 2006. It was the best day and the worst day of my life.

Just before I handed my firearms into the armoury I tidied my locker and gave it a spring clean and for some strange reason an odd thought ran through my head: "I won't need this for a while." – a strange idea to float randomly through my brain considering I was on Firearms again in the morning.

Anyway I carried on with the day, I put the Glock 17 pistol, the

G36 carbine and Taser away in the armoury and said goodbye to the shift with the usual banter 'until the morning.'

I walked back to my fragrant locker to place my body armour, tac vest and belt rig away and the thought came back again: "Keep it tidy." It reminded me of when I was told to change my underpants as a kid just in case I got run over. I left the station and made the 15-mile journey home to be greeted by my son and my partner.

I was settling down for a quiet evening, what could possibly go wrong? It was around 7.10 and I had been home less than three minutes when I found out.

It was then I heard a loud bang and noise of a car revving and screaming at the front of our house. A driver had decided to park his car in the front of our house, actually inside the house. It had come through the wall.

I can still remember, there was the smell of exhausts, a smell of rubber and this horrendous engine noise constantly revving.

The training kicked in and I went into rescue mode. I got to the passenger side of the car and looked at the young man at the wheel. The first thing I remember was that this threw me slightly. He was so young. For some reason I thought the driver was going to be someone elderly who lost control of a car and had a mishap. This was not that person. No, this was some little tyke who, as I later found, had been at a funeral wake all day, was drunk, decided to go looking for more beer. He stole a car and then lost control. That car was the car now sitting in front of me.

I was in police mode and my instincts kicked right in. I tried to help this fellow out of the vehicle. My right hand was clenched. I desperately tried to persuade him to take his foot of the accelerator but he wouldn't.

Now here comes the weird bit. I get the idea, and it was a firm knowing, that if I wrap my hand around the seat belt, my extra super powers will mean I can stop the car if it moves.

Oh yeah! Great idea! That was the first fail of the day. The car had been wedged on a shattered wall. It now fell down from that shattered wall, hit the floor and careered backwards with me attached to it via the seat belt. I could now feel myself slowly getting dragged under the car until eventually the front wheel dragged my feet in. Now at this point I realised this wasn't going to be fun and held on as long as I could until the front wheel sucked me in and under it.

I can remember everything going bright red. My legs were in a bad way as I rolled out from the sump. At this point I thought, 'You lucky bugger,' and desperately pulled myself out of the path of the car. Then I was hit by the car again, and this time I was under the bumper.

I can't remember much after this to be honest except I had this moment of asking: "Am I dead or paralysed?" I was so disassociated from my body, I didn't know. I don't mean this spiritually; I meant, I felt disconnected, I didn't know where my body was or what it was doing.

Meanwhile, the driver had decided he didn't want any more of this. He left me for dead and fled the scene, driving off into the distance. I remember faces screaming at me and being pulled around by family, neighbours and then the paramedics. Then I faded out again.

Next came the most surreal moment of all. I woke up in James Paget Hospital in Great Yarmouth, with the Deputy Chief Constable of Suffolk holding my hand. You can't dream that sort of thing!

Even as I am writing this, all these years later, I am struck by just how strange it is. So I am going to recap on events up to this point. One minute I'm at home, with some poxy soap opera on in the background.

Then the wall comes in.

Next revving engines, pain, reality check.

Then in hospital holding my boss's hand.

At the time it was all too much and I went back to sleep.

Back in the outside world, the UK's finest are out there doing their job, and have located the driver hiding in a field several miles away.

For me back in the hospital, I was in for a long haul. The weeks moved on and I come to realise I am in all types of trouble.

The list of physical injuries is frightening. I'm alive but with damage to leg, back, arms, face, head, and feet. I have a snapped Achilles tendon, broken ankles and shoulder injuries.

But I'm fine, or so I say.

Months tick by and the injuries heal – just the odd limp after 6 months of rehabilitation. I'm back, I'm there, or so I thought.

I had been on several drugs for pain relief during this time notably Tramadol, Pregabalin, paracetamol and God knows what else. Then, as I weaned myself off them something dramatic happened to me. I had changed.

I loved life and (apart from 12 years in the British Army!) I was normal, life was great. That had been me and I expected to just pick up where I had left off.

But it wasn't like that. Now it felt different, I was becoming agitated, aggressive, nervous and reclusive. I was a happy go lucky sort of guy. This is how I had always seen myself.

Now I was feeling hatred and I mean hatred. The drugs I had been taking in my physical recovery had masked these new feelings; numbed them and shoved to the back of my subconscious.

I couldn't sleep and there were what I came to call 'naughty noises'. These were shouts and screams in my head (and sometimes out loud) which went on through the night. And the night was accompanied by this horrendous impending doom. So I go to a new friend that I knew would help, Jack Daniels. Jack Daniels, Tramadol and Pregabalin to be precise – that managed to keep the naughty noises at bay. But even at this low point I knew that this was no solution. I needed to get out of this place. And I did. I did it, and this book is the result. It is what I learned and how I used that. It took time, changes, learning new things, doing things in a different way. It changed me, my life and what I do. My whole life direction and my career are now totally different. Now, I help others, especially those in the uniformed services, to heal after traumatic incidents.

I said the car came through the wall was the best and worst day of my life. So, why was it the best? Well without it happening I wouldn't have learned everything I now know about trauma and how to heal it. I wouldn't have developed a new way of helping people deal with trauma, I wouldn't have helped myself and then gone on to help others. And I'm still doing it. This is my first book. And I really hope that if you have been in this place it can help you. So read on to find out what happened next and what the next can be for you.

No D in PTSD

Life in uniform: what does a uniform mean and how does it affect those who wear it?

If you are in the uniformed service people will see you in a certain way and you will pick this up. Your job also means you are likely to face traumatic situations on a regular basis. Here I take a look at what a uniform means, to you and to those you serve.

In this chapter I'm going to look at what it means to live your life in uniform – the ups and the downs, what's special and what's hard. We all exist, think and react in our own environment and our uniform is part of that. So if we understand it better we can prepare and protect ourselves.

So what is a uniform? On one level uniforms are everywhere – banks, supermarkets, school uniform, traffic wardens they all wear a uniform, to give a sense of a corporate identity, and to make the wearer easy to recognise. But there is a more special meaning and signal of a uniform, that worn by what are usually called 'uniformed services'. Here we mean something different. We're talking about an "elite" group including:

○ The armed forces
○ Police services
○ Ambulance services
○ Fire service
○ Coastal rescue services

People wearing these uniforms invest a lot in this identity. Being part of this group is usually a considered decision and often the result of a long-held wish to join a certain profession.

So, if you've joined one of these forces or services, you've probably been asked the question on more than one occasion: "Why would you do that?"

The answer to that question varies for each individual, but some of the most common reasons are:

○ Job security – soldiers, police, firefighters and paramedics are always going to be needed. And they get a pension.
○ To help people – if you give this answer, you probably feel kind of stupid when you say it. But actually it's the most common reason for people going into uniform. You know you can't save the world in a Superman sort of way (was that another career choice, Superhero?), but you really do want to make a difference.
○ New experiences – you'll get to do things you could never do in an ordinary job, get away from the boring world

that is your life, and they'll pay you as well!
- Training and education – you want to learn new skills that you can use now and when you're back out on civvy street.
- It's something different – as they say, "It's not your average 9 to 5".
- The uniform is cool – well, no answer to that one.

I'm not saying any of these answers are right or wrong, I'm just giving some people's version of events. You might recognise your reasons in any or all of the above.

If you are serving in one of the uniformed services maybe, you look at yourself and think "Yeah, it's everything I wanted". Or maybe you look back at your reasons for joining up in the first place and laugh yourself silly at your naivety, especially if you've been in the service for a while. Truth is, you probably think both of them – and swing between one and the other depending on the sort of day you've had.

Above, I listed a whole number of positive reasons for being in the service and the positive emotions around it. All the above are true about being in uniformed service, but depending on which service you're in, the statements below are true too:

- Some days are just plain boring, with lots of waiting around and no action.
- There's always someone higher up who'll notice what you do wrong but not what you do right.
- The hours are crap – you're working shifts, missing parties, being away from home for weeks or months at a time.
- There's endless paperwork and admin.

○ Not everyone appreciates your efforts – you get spat at, abused, assaulted, and maybe shot at.
○ You'll have to do things you really don't want to, sometimes things that go completely against your nature or your moral code.
○ Some days will be stressful and/or awful.
○ Some days may be so stressful or awful, they'll feel like they've changed you forever.

Thing is, you knew when you joined up that this was the reality of it – or at least you knew in the abstract. People told you, common sense told you. But your reasons for joining overrode the reasons not to join. You can cope with those negatives, you told yourself, to get the benefits.

And that can work for a lot of the time. But, more than most jobs, working in the uniformed services can throw more at you than most people, working the average nine to five, ever have to cope with.

In reality, you never know what you can cope with until it appears on the horizon, and that's really what this book is about – coping, and how we all do it. It's about the things that you come up against that you weren't expecting, the circumstances that you have to deal with, and the times you have to go against your better judgement, or even your human instincts.

You're You, Not Your Uniform
That is the core message of this book. Because that's the thing. Behind every uniform is a human being with human frailties and human strengths. The uniform is worn on the outside, not the inside. The person inside has a personality of their own, and a history of experiences that naturally make them tend to act in a certain way, generally and to specific situations.

Psychologists will tell us that we all wear masks, changing them depending on the social interaction we're involved in. And this makes some sense if you think about it. You behave differently to your boss than to your love, or to the guy sitting across on the train? (I hope so, otherwise life could be really awkward for you!)

A uniform is like a full body mask
But the point is, behind those masks is still you. A uniform is like a full-body mask. It will make you act differently, maybe put your shoulders back a bit, be a bit more polite than you usually are. It will probably even make you feel different – you'll know this, perhaps you will feel more powerful, more respected? What we can say for certain is that it won't cancel out who you are.

You know that. But the people you are dealing with, civilians, don't always accept that. You don't have to watch TV, or read a paper, or Google news or whatever, for long before you'll see something about someone in uniform who's acted in a "bad" way. It provokes shock and outrage. And behind this lie a set of beliefs – "these people are trained to be different, they shouldn't react as other people do".

The fact is though, uniform or not, you are a person, and that leaves you in a very difficult and sometimes conflicted situation. And it matters. How people who you are serving see you affects how they behave and that will affect you.

As a quick aside, it's interesting that a lot of research has found that as emergency service uniforms become more "militarised", people's concept of the services has also changed. You'll know, if that's the sort of uniform you wear, that you can just as often be viewed as an "occupying force", out to control and subvert the citizens, as you are seen as someone whose role is "to protect and serve". This has brought new stresses to the role of emergency service worker.

This conflict between the person in the uniform and the person under it is never more apparent than in a situation where there's trauma, threat or catastrophe. You, as a uniformed person have to deal with it, it's part of your job. And the chances are you will deal with it at the time, as professionally as you can. But once the uniform comes off? How does the human being underneath the uniform cope and come to terms with their feelings and thoughts? How do you cope?

That's the real question, the one that we're going to investigate here. How does your body and your mind cope with this stress, and trauma, and what happens when your coping mechanisms don't work for you? What happens, and how will you deal with it when it does?

We've talked above about coping with trauma or catastrophe, as if it's one single event you'll have to deal with, like most people. But you're different. In the forces or emergency services you'll have to repeatedly cope with these things, on a day to day basis. Or else, especially if you're in the armed forces, stationed in a conflict zone, you'll be in a position where the threat is there for days, weeks or even months at a time.

That's a lot to ask of anyone. So we are going to look at how you can protect yourself later in the book.

Often talked about, seldom understood. A brief history of mental illness in the armed services

Mental problems caused by exposure to traumatic events are nothing new – they have been talked about at least as far back as the Ancient Greeks But effective treatment has been rare. Here's a quick run through

Post Traumatic Stress Disorder isn't some sort of new-fangled illness that's come around in modern times.

As long as people have been fighting wars and being at catastrophic events, there is evidence of its psychological effects on the individuals.

As early as 490 BC, Herodotus, a Greek historian, was documenting evidence from the battle of Marathon. He talks of an Athenian fighter who became permanently blind after the soldier standing beside him was killed – even though he himself was completely untouched. Nowadays, this is known as a conversion reaction.

Some time on from there, in 1678, physicians linked to the Swiss army gave a name to the group of behaviours they saw in soldiers who had experienced the trauma of battle and were affected psychologically by it – they called it "nostalgia" and believed it was related to soldiers missing home. German doctors noticed the same thing around the same time, calling it "heimweh", they believed that it was an effect of the soldier missing home and being caught up in memories of it.

Quite how they linked lack of appetite, sleep disorders, heart palpitations and dissociative behaviour to being merely homesick isn't clear!

But the idea was obviously having a moment – the French gave it similar meaning, calling it "maladie du pays".

The Spanish description of "estar roto" (to be broken) may have been closer to the truth – these men seemed to be, psychologically at least, broken men.

Diaries and journals have always been a useful way of gathering historical information, and in 1727, during the siege of Gibraltar, a soldier who was involved in the defence of the city used his journal to document some interesting insights on the state of the military men.

He talked of soldiers deliberately injuring themselves. He mentioned several cases of suicide among the troops, and highlighted the effects of the extreme physical exhaustion that left some soldiers unwilling or unable to process simple instructions or follow orders, even if the result was a whipping. These same soldiers often showed an unwillingness to eat, drink or work in any way.

In an early effort to categorise the symptoms rather than just describe them, a French surgeon, Larrey, talked of three progressive stages of the condition (which we now know as PTSD):

o An increased imagination and heightened state of excitement
o A time of fever and gastrointestinal upheaval and symptoms
o Frustration and depression.

During the American Civil War, the medical staff saw many cases of soldiers left scarred by the effects of war – paralysis, "the shakes", self-harming, and severe palpitations (which came to be known as soldier's heart) were all noted. Another thing noticed at this time was a tendency for apparently well soldiers to return home after fighting and then completely collapse, showing many of the psychological disturbances seen by the doctors in the battle arena.

With such a long history, it's surprising that it wasn't until 1905 that mental collapse and all the associated psychological and physical symptoms were seen as being a direct consequence of the stress of war, and as being a legitimate medical condition.

We have the Russians to thank for this insight, a result of their experiences fighting against the Japanese. This led to the start of the field of military psychiatry. Their belief in the importance of delivering treatment for the condition close to the front line, and then getting the men back to fighting, is still held today by many military psychiatric teams. Why this belief was picked up on and carried forward isn't clear, since during the Russian conflict less than 20 percent who received treatment close to the front eventually returned to the battle. In other words, it wasn't very successful.

Shell Shock

Amazingly, in spite of all this evidence, and the Russians' enlightened approach (or maybe because it *was* the Russians), the First World War saw the first use of the phrase "Shell Shock" to describe the group of conditions that were seen in some troops. Myers, in 1915, introduced the phrase (although there is some evidence that he "borrowed" the phrase from soldiers themselves, where it seems to have been in use already). He used it to explain what happened when men had been near a shell as it exploded, and how they suffered physical damage to the brain and nervous system. When it was pointed out that many suffering the symptoms of confusion, being dazed, or exhibiting what was to become known as "the thousand-yard stare" had never been near a shell when it exploded, these soldiers were labelled as being cowardly or weak – a convenient label.

If you take a look at some of the photographs taken of soldiers at the time it makes it clear. One which always gets me, is this one (you can download it at www.rarehistoricalphotos.com/shell-shocked-soldier-1916).

When you consider that the convention of the time was to be solemn when photographs were taken, this photo shows starkly what the face of "madness" could look like. Looking at the photo and the conditions, it's incredible to think that the powers that be didn't think that living like that could have mental or emotional consequences.

There were some voices at the times who did acknowledge the dreadful psychological effects, and who gave it a description. Here is as an effective description of what we now call PTSD as anyone has ever written. It is by G E Smith and T Pear in their work *Shell Shock and its Lessons, 1917:*

"Whatever may be the state of mind of the patient immediately after the mine explosion, the burial in the dug-out, the sight and sound of his lacerated comrades, or other appalling experiences which finally incapacitate him for service in the firing line, it is true to say that by the time of his arrival in a hospital in England, his reason and his senses are usually not lost but functioning with painful efficiency. His reason tells him quite correctly, and far too often for his personal comfort, that had he not given, or failed to carry out, a particular order, certain disastrous and memory-haunting results might not have happened. It tells him, quite convincingly, that in his present state he is not as other men are. Again, the patient reasons, quite logically, but often from false premises, that since he is showing certain symptoms which he has always been taught to associate with 'madmen,' he is mad too, or on the way to insanity."

Different terms: same condition
So throughout history, what we now call PTSD has been identified using different terms. Here are some of the most common which have been used in relatively recent history.

- **Lack of moral fibre** was introduced by the British Royal Air Force at the beginning of World War II to stigmatise and discharge aircrew that refused to fly missions without a medical excuse. For the British Royal Air Force use, see Edgar Jones, "'LMF': The Use of Psychiatric Stigma in the Royal Air Force During the Second World War," Journal of Military History 70 (2006): 439–58.
- **Shell shock** was first used by Charles Myers in 1915 in a *Lancet* article. Also by Frederick Mott in 1919
- **Combat exhaustion/combat fatigue** – these terms were used in both World War Two and in Vietnam

○ **Stress response syndrome** – This was first coined in 1952 in the American Psychological Associations's Diagnostic and Statistical Manual of Mental Disorders (DSM-I), this is the first acknowledgement that it was stress that played the major part in the condition.

Section 2

In this section , I feature people who work in environments where they can suffer PTSD. Although, as you will see, there are an increasing number of support services on offer, we still have a long way to go. Many of the people I spoke to have found talking therapies such as hypnotherapy helps to fix the problems. I hope you enjoy reading their stories and realising you are not alone.

No D in PTSD

Stories from the frontline

A STORY FROM THE UNITED STATES: IT STARTED WITH A HURRICANE

Hi, I'm Stephen Watts Junior Patrol Shift Supervisor at Jackson Parish Sheriff's Office, USA, where I have 15 years' service and as you will see I have learned a lot about trauma over the years.

Suffering after a traumatic incident is almost a taboo subject because it implies you are having certain problems or thoughts. There is almost a stigma around even mentioning it if you are having problems sleeping or if you are having nightmares or any of the sort of stuff which can go on. If it comes up at all it usually comes up in the form of humour. Guys will make a joke about it or get humour in the everyday stuff. From working with guys for years you will find out that what they are joking about is, a lot of times, where their problems are. They are making comedy out of whatever is bothering them. There is some help out there but it sometimes doesn't work that well. So, take an example, say a police involved shooting or some sort of death-related incident happens, they will bring in counsellors, but it's done in a group setting. Multiple people are there and the way that it is organised it doesn't allow the person to keep their privacy or dignity. I don't think that is the best model. So, if a guy or a girl who feels they need something extra they are not in an environment to actually say anything. There is a lot of peer pressure to not admit what is going on, to not explore whatever these things are that you are going through.

There is a crisis intervention team, I have been part of that, it's quite loosely organised and they will call some of these guys in to see if they can help. But like a lot of things if you wave them off they leave. If you go through something traumatic the chances are that any problems will not come up immediately because you are so busy with what happened.

So here, immediately after an incident they are going to take your gun away from you, it's going to be evidence and everything is going to be investigated as a crime scene. Within a certain amount of time you are going to have to give a statement and you are going to go through an investigation process which for a lot of officers is going to be extremely weird as they are going to be on the other end of it now, it's a strange place to be in for those guys.

Nowadays, in the States, and this is probably true anywhere, anything like that is going to be a very public thing. I come from an area which is a tight-knit community so if there is a police involved shooting, the entire community is going to know that it happened, who did it, who was involved with it and probably a lot of details about it which they should not know. There is a lot of exposure via social media and all the stuff that goes along with that. This means the individual officer is not only having to go through the stress of how it is affecting his work, he is also having to go through the stress of how it is affecting his family.

In the department, we know each other pretty well, so there is the ability for someone to get support within the close-knit unit and this happens. But outside of that, there is no policy or procedure to get them anything. I'm sure that the sheriff's office would try to help in any way they could, but it would be based off of their goodwill only, not on policy.

Because we work in a rural area we essentially wear a whole lot of different hats. An officer here will have different jobs that he will do as routine, which in a bigger place would be more specialised. In a bigger place if there is a murder or something traumatic like that, the individual street officer's exposure is likely to be very slim. Ours is very much greater -- suicides, murders, car fatalities things of that nature, you are exposed to them all. Since I have been here you are looking at numerous suicides; a half a dozen murders; and so many car fatalities I cannot count. One of the car fatalities was my uncle, my father's brother. I was there when that happened.

A thing which really affected me was Hurricane Katrina in 2005. We were sent to New Orleans for a week. It was traumatic for lots of officers who got sent there. There were a lot of fatalities; police were getting shot at for trying to help. There was lots of looting. It was a United States city being turned into a 3rd world country overnight. That has been downplayed since, but it did happen. I was there and I saw it.

It was a big event for me, as such a young officer at the time. It was one of the biggest chaotic events which happened outside of basic police work. There were a lot of bad things. A lot of corruption was exposed. We saw officers doing things they were not supposed to do – things which were not acceptable. In this situation you can lose respect for certain people. You see people from within your own state, from within your own country change into people you do not recognise. This is hard, I know that when I got back home anxiety became an issue for me straight away.

A strange thing happened then which I have later found out is common. I was glad to get home and rest, but at the same time I wanted to go back. It was weird, this thing which is disturbing you is the thing you want to go back to and get in the middle of it again. It's so odd.

Then there is the contrast. There, where the hurricane happened was a chaotic environment, with the infrastructure gone, for example there was no electricity and little running water. But then four hours north back at home, everything seems normal. But it is not normal in your head. I found myself at work, riding around expecting something to happen, but it is not there.

I was extremely anxious and everything seemed a potential threat. It really was finding monsters in the shadows. Other people began to pick up there was something wrong, especially after I had a few drinks and let my guard down. The emotions really came into play at that point.

I was single and just 21 at the time. So I could hide how I felt a lot of the time. With my friends hanging out at weekends I could usually hide it. I was only around my sister, her kids, my mother and my friends for a bit of time, none saw me all the time so that it meant I could hide my feelings. You can get pretty good at hiding stuff when you don't want people to ask questions.

I did want help though, I wanted to help myself. I had started looking into hypnosis several years back as I was trying to pull myself out of a rut. I started with NLP in an attempt to fix some of the struggle going on inside. Rather than going to see a therapist I self-taught, learning about different modalities, learning how to fix this stuff that was going on with me unconsciously. I wanted to fix the stuff which was going on without making a big deal about it. That was what was going on with me unconsciously.

I don't run a business as a hypnotherapist. For me it is personal. I studied hypnotherapy with Mike Mandel and never looked back. I don't want to call it a hobby because it is a more than that. I have used it with the guys at work. The guys that want help they will come to me. I've got different modalities that I can help them with.

I am always known as the guy who is reading and learning. I have always had a learner's mentality. When I started getting into hypnosis I was very cautious about who I told. Especially in the south of the United States, the religious element is strong and often has negative opinions of hypnotherapy that are not rooted in reality but in fiction. I studied online and joined the Mike Mandel hypnosis academy online. When I made the decision to go to Toronto to a hypnosis conference I don't think I told anyone what I was doing.

When I got back I talked to some of the guys on my shift, some of the guys I was close to, so they knew what I was doing. They were interested, and a lot of it was they were almost wanting magic tricks. My approach has always been helping myself and how I can help other people.

So, I approached it from a very selfish viewpoint about how I could fix my problems. Then people would come with phobia or one guy had problems with forgetfulness. Sometimes they don't really believe that you could help, don't really believe you so you have to convince them. You have to put on your convincer hat then. With those guys, little interventions count; things like making people's hiccups stop, making headaches go away. All this adds a level of credibility and then they are ready to take the next step. The word spreads and then you have a guy walking up to you on break and it's 'hey man can you help me with this.' One of the things is anonymity, giving those guys the ability to come to you and when they trust you in that regard it helps. I don't want to let my boss down, but I would much rather let my boss down than let one of the guys beside me down. If you are true to that, you almost never run into issues with the above people.

And the help is needed, we all know that when we work in these services.

PTSD is an accumulation of events that come over time and with some of them you don't even know consciously that it is affecting you. There is a lot of things that can cause problems: if you see a dismembered body or unattended death even if you don't have a personal connection with that person there is almost an element of humanity which makes is so tough. Is it that we were not supposed to see fellow humans in that condition? That builds up over a period of time, and the way that I see it is that it is better to take the garbage out before it is full than allow it to overflow and stink up the whole house.

If I wanted to do this helping officially, I would have to go to the higher ups which I feel is an issue: it may well be that what is going on is not necessarily any of their business. If you are performing and you are mentally fit to do your job, then fine. It is often not black and white. People like to look at stuff as if it is either broken or it is fixed but that is not how it works.

If a level of help exists where we could call an anonymous hotline then even I don't know about it, so that level of support, if it exists is not well known. The crisis intervention programme I worked with is not perfect. They work in groups, which is often not ideal, and they work to a script which often does not fit.

I favour a different approach. Get people off on their own where I can talk to them. I have done that with guys even over things such as problems at home. When you are a supervisor over a group of guys you have to really watch out for them. You may need to take time to pull them off to the side and see where they are at. If there are major red flags then I will have to report it to the higher ups and say this guy needs to be pulled off for a little bit. I have no doubt that they get such a guy help, but the actual path is unknown to me because it is not really told to us.

No D in PTSD

Stories from the frontline

NURSES, DOCTORS, POLICE: SIMILAR ISSUES AND SOME WAYS FORWARD

Emergency nurse

I have worked as a nurse in A and E for years and I enjoy it. Or I used to enjoy it. The increasing workload has got crazy and I spend most of my time feeling bad because I don't have time to care. I had been feeling like this for ages then I had a dreadful weekend where there had been a road traffic accident involving a child. When I went off shift I couldn't get it out of my mind. Over the next few days I keep getting flashbacks and feeling ill.

I ended up going off sick. I am back at work now after having some sessions of hypnotherapy and some CBT. It has really helped but I think that with more support and especially if the work hadn't had been so pressured I would never have got in this state in the first place.

Police Officer

I was diagnosed with PTSD and put on long term sick leave a year ago. Before this happened, I had always thought that PTSD was something which happened after one traumatic event – I think of things like the 7/7 bombings in London or a crowd disaster. I now know that this is not true, and it wasn't what happened to me. What happened to me was much more slow burn. The department I worked in was horrible, lots of back-biting and politics. It was a blame culture so we were all always worried about the bosses coming down like a ton of bricks for any mistake. It all came to a head when we were even more understaffed than usual. I was coming off shift and then feeling like there was no break at all. In the end, I just cracked. I couldn't take any more.

I had some CBT, but I had to wait a while. I left the police in the end, which was a shame as I loved the job.

Police officer about a colleague

I had known John (not his real name) for years and we were really good mates. We'd trained together and rose up the ranks together. I knew something was up when he bought a new car and started driving like a maniac. I tried to reason with him, he of all people should know the dangers, he's been to enough RTAs over the years! Also, just personally, he put his career under such risk. I talked to his wife and she was worried, she said John wasn't sleeping as well. In the end, I did finally get John to open up. We had been dealing with a really violent dangerous guy. John had seen first-hand the damage this guy had done and was eaten up with the fact that he was still on the streets. I did persuade John to get to occupational health and he had some therapy. But he says that the best thing was his talks with me, being able to open up to someone who had been there and did understand. I feel proud of that. I just wish we saw more of it. I know most people wouldn't have had that sort of relationship.

Junior doctor
I always wanted to be a doctor and I was so pleased when I got into med school. A few years later I was in a mess. We were so busy, often I didn't drink water on my shift as I knew I wouldn't have time to go the loo. Nothing single happened, there was no one event which pushed me over the edge, it was a slow build up. Symptoms were not sleeping, not eating, drinking too much alcohol when I was off shift, giving up hobbies, breaking up with my partner. In the end I went for hypnotherapy and it really helped. I learned techniques for 'switching off' I also learned how to be more assertive to get a bit more time off work. I now try to help younger colleagues when I see them in trouble, but I feel I shouldn't have to – there should be more help from the NHS out there and they should look after us more.

No D in PTSD

Stories from the frontline: WG a serving soldier

BANTER CAN HELP . . .SO CAN HYPNOTHERAPY

As a serving soldier, I have experiences of mates who have been in trouble. One in particular springs to mind, I am a practising hypnotherapist as well as a soldier and I am going to tell you the reason I got into hypnotherapy. I was already performing street and stage hypnosis when I found out a good friend, also a soldier, had PTSD as a result of an operational tour.

The thing which was surprising was that, although I knew this guy well, I didn't realise there was anything up with him. It wasn't until he had been through the whole thing and actually got medication that I noticed something was up – I noticed the effects of the medication rather than the PTSD itself and that is interesting in itself.

It was a big change, he went from being a very smooth slick soldier to forgetting the sort of things that he always knew. It was very noticeable and I believe that this forgetfulness was down to the drugs which he was prescribed.

Of course, in our line of work forgetfulness can be very dangerous and this is often why people can end up getting laid off. Although, in some situations it should be that we can do something before this stage is reached. So I learned that PTSD can go undetected, even among close friends. I know also now that PTSD can start in all sorts of different ways, it doesn't have to be one traumatic event

PTSD can be hard to spot
One thing does seem to be common with PTSD in the military – a problem starts when an event happens which someone couldn't control. After the event, this analytical thing sets in. The 'what ifs' the 'if I had done . . ' The 'if only' – those running thoughts which will not stop, it can be like a loop in the head, all those running thoughts – what if this didn't happen and that other thing had happened.

This is something we all experience I suppose, I know I do. But then sometimes you can see it is becoming a bit obsessional, a bit it won't go away. It can reach the stage where the soldier starts getting really strong visions or flashbacks. If that happens, then it is definitely the time you need to be looking or asking for help.

So that's one way PTSD can develop, but it is not the only one. PTSD doesn't just come down to events from operations, it can be just a cumulative thing. Or it can be terrible life events away from operations.

I had a friend who discovered his mother dead when he came back on R&R (rest and recuperation) – he was back from a tour and went around to knock on his mother's door and found her dead. His only method of resolving this was to get back out on tour to be with his section, taking his mind off the situation, and I have heard that this is a common coping mechanism.

Coping in the military

One of the best, in my eyes, about being in the army is the natural camaraderie. In the army I do see a natural coping mechanism. Especially in the infantry you find the guys just want to be with their muckers, be with the guys they have trained with. I am different being REME (Royal Electrical Mechanical Engineers) so I don't have those close regular ties, but I do see them as I work.

In the infantry, they are much closer and the camaraderie or brotherhood for each other is great. They support each other in a very special way. What seems to make the difference is the natural banter that the military have. You see people who know how to tease to the level that feels positive and supporting. It is just natural. And a lot of soldiers will be going through the same thing at any one time. The banter means it can get laughed off. I think a lot of natural resolution can come through that. It's not much talked about and outsiders don't know it goes on, but it does and it matters.

At the same time this doesn't mean that the problems will always get spotted. Sometimes you can see that someone who is in trouble and sometimes you can't. A lot can be hidden and that is something we need to be looking at and there are some great things going on.

Trauma Risk Management (TRiM)

I have recently completed the army's course on trauma risk management (Trim) and I think it is one thing which the army is doing very well. The really good thing about it is that they get to the person who has suffered the trauma within the first 24 hours, and then checking them later, first a week then at longer intervals. As a trained person, who is there to go through the TRiM process with them, you can then see how they are reacting. When you see them later you can check and see what the difference is, so you will be keeping an eye out for things such as if they are having more alcohol or are they clearly not sleeping. The other thing which is great about it is how natural the chat is, it just fits into the way soldiers talk to each other anyway. It is delivered in a relaxed environment with not too many prying questions. This allows you to build more of a judgement as to how the person in coping, rather than digging deeper for a reaction to the situation.

Because of this you can be very relaxed about asking questions about how they are post the incident and seeing how they react, you can tell a lot more about a person through this. It's trying to identify the invisible coping mechanisms.

It is a fantastic system, and I think it is a real breakthrough which is becoming more widely used in other services, I know that the police are using it as well now. It is a good tool in the right hands as well.

Hypnosis to help
So that is the good stuff, but I think we still have a long way to go to change attitudes. There is still too much of the 'man up', get on with it, don't talk about it. It is changing massively but we need to do more. You are an even bigger man if you man up and tell someone – that's the message.

Knowing hypnosis has helped me over last 10 years and I would love to show my fellow soldiers how much it can help them. I know that through the regular use of hypnosis my thought processes are different. I am not so hung up on stuff, I am much better at not allowing things to bother me. If something bothers me on one day now it is wiped out on the next day.

If I get my way and manage to introduce hypnosis to the military, I will be very happy. There are some great services out there, such as Help for Heroes, Band of Brothers/Sister and I know the work of Tedworth House and think it is such a positive thing. It would be even better with such a powerful tool like hypnosis in regular use that should be available to every soldier who wants it. I know like any treatment it will not work for everyone, but from my experience there is a greater number of people it does work for than doesn't.

No D in PTSD

Stories from the frontline: Bob Burness

AN AMBULANCE SERVICE BENEFITS FROM HYPNOSIS

I am used to traumatic situations. I did 29 years in the fire service with all the problematic jobs you go to.

We have had a very good coping strategy back then which over the years has dropped away. Our sense of humour if you had a bad job kept you going. You would go back and have a water fight, or you would take the mickey out of each other with all sorts of practical jokes. Over the years, these things got banned. Certain managers didn't like them and classed them as bullying, it was frowned on and reduced and eventually stopped completely. Often the jokes and the banter wasn't funny if you took it out of context, but at the time they relieved the pressure and were a very useful and active tool and had been for many years. Towards the end of my time in the fire service, I was actually a CBRN (chemical, biological, radioactive, nuclear incidents) officer. This meant I would go out to big scale disasters so I learnt a lot more about the nasty stuff which is going on out there in the world. This does tend to depress you a bit. I left the fire brigade and joined the ambulance service and I have been with them for just over nine years. Obviously, in this job you get exposed to the horrors which go on out there but it is a different culture to the fire service. There is only you and your one colleague in the vehicle or occasionally you are on your own, so there is no way of having that banter, no way of having that pressure relief.

Shifts add to the pressure
Because of the pressures of work as soon as you have finished one horrible job you are off to the next job which may or may not be a necessary job. You can go from holding someone's hand as they die to dealing with a drunk or someone with a cut finger. You have to be able to switch from someone who is in a really bad place to self-inflicted silliness with drinking too much and the like. That can be very hard to do and you will be getting that day in day out and it wears you down.

This is where a lot of ambulance people get the equivalent of PTSD. It's a cumulative effect. Some do get the really bad jobs, and then you might get the single incident which sparks a problem but for the vast majority it is the cumulative effect.

Then there are the shifts, you are doing 12, 13, 14 hour shifts because the start and the finish don't always go to plan. You are then coming back shortly afterwards to do it all over again and it wears you out. So, your resistance is low, you then get a few silly jobs and you do end up really struggling.

My own experience is that I had had a bad year. I had a lung cancer scare. I was expecting life changing consequences or worse. In the end, the doctors just removed the tumour and said 'fine you're sorted, off you go'. It should have been a relief, but was a hell of a shock.

Immediately following that I was doing some DIY in the house I got electrocuted and ended up in hospital and a couple of days after that my dog got attacked by a pit bull.

Bit of a meltdown
So, I had a bit of a meltdown, something I never thought would happen to me, I had always been 'you just deal with things practically and move on.' But I got to the point where I literally couldn't move, as I sat in the bedroom trying to get ready for work, I could not even get my trousers on. I just sat there completely stunned. I saw the doctor and his only solution was to give me some tablets and send me away. I managed, with the help of a few friends, to survive the next few weeks and then I started looking into how to get myself back together again and get it sorted.

I did this mainly through meditation and self-hypnosis. There was nobody local who specialises in PTSD hypnosis type stuff and I am not a fan of Skype, I like face to face or not at all.

It took a while, but I got myself pretty much sorted. Then in January I got assaulted, head butted by a patient while defending one of my colleagues. The press got hold of it and made a big story of it. So, for the following three weeks a couple of times a day I would have to relive it with the press asking: oh tell us about the attack, how did that make you feel?

As I tell all my clients we learn by repetition. This happened to me, the press made me repeat the incident time and time again, I was asked things like; 'look at this photo of the incident, what does that remind you of?' It really screwed me over in my head at a time I thought I was reasonably okay. I realised later that it was all that repetition that caused a bigger problem than the actual attack. So again, I went back to my meditations and my self-hypnosis. I also used binaural beats, which is another form of meditation. But it took me a long time to get better, because my problems had been so well reinforced in the aftermath. I suffered the classic signs and symptoms of PTSD. And then I went to a similar sort of call – a young male known to be violent had collapsed. We got there and it was so similar to the previous incident, it was almost like a re-enactment.

I froze. Luckily, my colleague knew my history and he took the lead in what we were doing and between us we got the problem solved, but it did make me question whether or not I could continue the job in the ambulance service. I then went into doing more meditations and other therapies. I found an online eye movement techniques related to EDMR (see page 86 in this book). I blasted all the therapies and eventually got it sorted by just keeping plodding away. It probably would have been more effective had I seen someone like Karl Smith, but there is no one around here who does that sort of thing.

My hypnosis work with the ambulance service
Work is my hiding place, all the jobs I have done have routines and protocols and you are always busy. So, you have to keep going, you don't get time to think about internal stuff.

Within the ambulance service we have SALS (Staff Advice and Support Liaison) and I actually work for them now having helped my crewmates out with hypnosis. It started when one of my mates just said: 'you are good at this hypnosis do you reckon you could help so and so out?' The guy had been off sick with stress for eight weeks. I saw him for one session and he went back to work the following week. He said, 'Oh that's great, I'm ready to go back to work now,' and he didn't have a problem after that at all.

Prior to that they only offered him counselling and mediation which hadn't worked for this guy. So SALS contacted me. They asked me if I would carry on doing my hypnosis and I said yes. It is all a bit under the radar as the HR department says they don't officially support hypnosis but then they say: 'here's the names of some people we would like you to see.'

The logic of management. Hypnotherapy is not accepted as a mainstream solution, while they openly support counselling, but they also accept that I am quite successful.

I put my name out there and got myself known in the West Midlands area. The West Midlands Ambulance Service covers a great expanse going out to Hereford and Worcester and Staffordshire, so some are too far away to see me. Nearer in the actual West Midlands I have seen dozens of people, and they all leave me, even after the first session, so much lighter. Some come back six months later saying I've had a bit of a wobble, no problem we work on that. The number of people I see varies a lot, ranging from two or three a month up to nine a month.

Rapid induction and Kinetic Shift

I use rapid hypnosis, Kinetic Shift, and some content free techniques. Often, I have no idea what their issues are and some of the time even they are not that certain. Basically, you help the client let go of all the memories they no longer want to hold onto and then you backfill with self-esteem, confidence and other feel-good stuff. It tends to work very well.

I always tell my clients from the ambulance service: 'I am not here to get you back to work, I am just here to get you into a good place to decide if you want to go back to work or not. I don't work for the management, I don't work for anyone other than you.'

This seems to be received rather well. I just wish there were more people prepared to learn the skills I have got so we could spread this through all the emergency services.

No D in PTSD

Section 3

In this section some of my valued colleagues talk about
therapies which can help. The first is Kinetic Shift, a
process developed by me to treat PTSD and other
conditions. I would then like to introduce you to:

Kevin Laye who has developed a process called Psy-Tap
designed to change how we hold memories

Dr Sue Peacock an expert in pain who uses the eye
movement technique Eye Movement Desensitisation and
Reprogramming

Dr Mark Chambers, a general practitioner and
hypnotherapist who uses Neuro Linguistic Programming to
help his clients deal with trauma and painful memories.

Alan Freeman a hypnotherapist and cognitive behavioural
expert

Liz Sharpe a hypnotherapist who also uses counselling
techniques

No D in PTSD

Get it sorted 1: Karl Smith writes

KINETIC SHIFT

I am a former soldier and a former police officer so I know what it is like to be on the front line. I've been to everywhere your travel agent won't send you. As a police officer I worked in counter-terrorism, as a firearms officer, so I know all about being under stress and under pressure.

I understand what it is like to have PTSD because I have been there. It was following my own experiences that I began on the journey which ended in me developing Kinetic Shift. After the traumatic experience I went through (which you can read about in Section One of this book) I was heavily medicated, especially with tramadol. Once I started to come off tramadol, all the PTSD which had been suppressed started coming out – anger, aggression, and that vaguer feeling that something wasn't right, I was feeling detached from the world. My doctor was starting to notice it too and I was pleading with him for more drugs.

Eighteen months after my traumatic experience I was back

at work but eating tramadol like smarties, just to feel alright –
to keep what I began to call the 'naughty noise' in my head under
control.

Colleagues at work were noticing, I wasn't the happy go lucky
bloke I had been before. A colleague suggested I try hypnosis.
The only experience I had of hypnosis up to that point was of a
stage hypnosis show I had seen at the seaside. So I said no, I don't
want any of that. But it was explained to me that it was a
powerful tool for change and it could help me, so I agreed to give
it a go.

I had a hypnotherapy session -- within 60 minutes everything
had changed. It was an amazing 60 minutes – the hypnotherapist
absolutely unravelled everything for me.

And there was a lot to unravel. I had compressed everything
I had seen in all the wars I has been involved in, from Northern
Ireland to the Balkans to Iraq, then I had moved to working on
the streets of the UK in very volatile situations. That is what PTSD
is, accumulated stress factors compressed and compressed. This
can go on for years, until the pressure reaches such a point that
it has to come out and that is when PTSD starts.

When it begins to unravel, it does so with a force behind it,
with a power. After that first 60-minute session, I spent nine
hours sobbing and crying, crying and sobbing. I was also laughing
– I was completely going backwards and forwards with all the
emotions pouring out. It was very strange – but that night I slept
like a baby for the first time that I could remember.

The best metaphor I can use is of a pressure cooker – those
old-fashioned ones with a valve on the top. It was as if the valve
had come off and all the steam was just pouring out.

The change the next day was profound and it changed my life.
Why I love what I do started then when I saw the power of
hypnosis and what it could achieve.

Active
Intuitive
Dynamic
Energising

Introduction to Kinetic Shift

It was the beginning of my journey to developing Kinetic Shift. I describe it in four words -- Active, Intuitive, Dynamic, Energising. I developed it by taking the best of the various hypnotic methods I learned in my training and ditching the useless ones. To develop Kinetic Shift I spent two years field testing it with the military and emergency services personnel.

Kinetic Shift is a way we can use your feelings and emotions, (or what we call your State) to change things. In Kinetic Shift we can work directly with the deeper mind, not with the cognitive part of the brain that will lie or cover up. Kinetic Shift has wonderful results for those suffering from Post-Traumatic Stress. It is nothing new, it uses techniques and insights which have been tried and tested elsewhere, for example eye movement techniques to process memories similar to those described in this book by Sue Peacock in her chapter on EMDR.

What *is* new about Kinetic Shift is how it is put together and the attitude of the people who are delivering it. This is partly because of my background, my time in the military and in the police, makes me very authoritarian so it is direct no-nonsense, let's get it sorted, no messing about.

And I like action – so do the other people I have trained to deliver Kinetic Shift. Kinetic Shift practitioners are lively – they are active, they will talk loudly, move about and change when they see you changing. It is all about responsiveness and working with your unique experience and how you see things. A Kinetic Shift session is above all an experience, and you need experience to change, don't you?

One thing that will definitely happen in a Kinetic Shift session is that you will know something has happened. That change, that release of the trauma, that unravelling will happen and you will know it. You will feel different. This can happen very quickly;

Kinetic Shift sessions are not timed. If you are better in 10 minutes – and this can happen – then that is great. Off you go!

So, what happens with Kinetic Shift?
So, let's start with what the problem, or your State, is. If you are suffering from trauma you will recognise this: you feel, but you can't express that feeling in words. You may even feel the words sticking in your throat and your throat tightening when you try to speak. You can't express and you feel stuck.

So here is the first surprise. In Kinetic Shift, we do not talk to that person, what's the point, we have already seen that you cannot answer, you cannot communicate. Instead we talk to the third person in the room, the unconscious mind, what I often call the 'monkey mind'. A Kinetic Shift practitioner will talk to that part very directly, very firmly and with the intention of sorting the problem.

So how do we get to that unconscious part, that 'monkey mind'? One thing Kinetic Shift uses is confusion. The idea is this – that the conscious logical mind, that 'stuck' part, is going to get in the way if it can, so one way of getting past it is to confuse it so it stops paying attention and allows the space for the Kinetic Shift practitioner to go directly to the 'monkey mind'.

We also use intuition. What we feel is often the best guide to where to go next. Intuition is something which we are frequently taught to ignore or play down, but in Kinetic Shift we listen to feelings and that begins to change things.

Another way of communicating when ordinary language fails us in through metaphors. Think about it, our early learning is through metaphors, fairy stories and tales in particular – going back to those can begin to clear those unhelpful memories and problems in PTSD. We can get a bit theatrical as well, to show you how your beliefs can hold you back and how powerful a belief can be in making you behave in certain ways. So, let's start changing those beliefs which are making you unhappy and holding you back. Those horrible physical feelings, flashbacks and painful emotions can be shifted and this can happen quickly.

Once that is achieved we can backfill and re-stock your memory – if you are suffering from trauma you have probably forgot what it feels like to be happy. Kinetic Shift uses techniques which can show you how to recreate happy memories and moments from your life so you get in touch with happiness again.

Because Kinetic Shift works dynamically and with each individual there is no one form which a session takes. That will depend on you and how you 'do' your problem. You will be observed so closely in a Kinetic Shift session – the practitioner is trained to pay attention, not just to what you say but to every movement and twitch which you make – we understand that you are communicating in many ways and they all count. You are unique and special and you will be made to feel special. And it's fun. You will feel yourself changing and the energy will be flowing back again.

You will not have to lie down, you will not be asked to close your eyes most of the time. You will be asked to move, make noise, participate and be very active.

The 7 stages of Kinetic Shift
1. Alert the State
2. Identify the State
Locate State (how do you feel it, where is it in your body, what does it look like and more)
Shift State (make it go somewhere else. If you can shift it you will know you are in control)
3. Eye Move It (EMIT) (use eye movement to process memories)
4. Back Fill. Go back to a happy time/place
5. Anchoring (fix that good State)
6. Calibrate/Test (make sure it is working, have the old bad feelings gone?)
7. Confusion (make sure that the new happier way is fixed in the 'monkey mind')

So if you think that is for you just get in contact and let's get it sorted.

I can be contacted at www.karlsmithhypnotherapy.com/

Get it Sorted 2: Kevin Laye writes

PSY-TAP (PSYCHOSENSORY TECHNIQUES AND PRINCIPLES)

PTSD, is a form of trauma, simple as that, and as such, should it be called a disorder? Let's look at traumatisation. Joseph LeDoux the neuroscientist says traumatisation requires a number of elements. The traumatising event itself, the meaning we give to the event, the level of our resilience in our brain and psychological state at the time of the event and most importantly the sense of real or perceived inescapability from the event.

All this happens often within an instant and leads to a fight or flight or a freeze response. If there is no fast resolution the Amygdala (basic part of the brain) 'holds on' to the event by moving it into the long-term memory, where it remains stored and in effect still 'active'. This happens even though the event has passed.

Humans have the capacity to ruminate and it is in these times when the events in a long-term memory can be brought into a working memory state and relive the trauma as though it is happening now, even though cognitively we know this is not the case.

The trauma is literally stuck in the right brain where we can catastrophise over it repeatedly because as far as the right brain is concerned it is happening now at a base neurological level. I call this the 'Stephen King Brain' where horrors can be recreated and embellished and amplified. There are many secondary emotional responses too such as: anger, rage, frustration, guilt, shame, depressive tendencies, and withdrawn or low moods.

Trying to manage these with traditional counselling, CBT or psychoanalysis are very ineffective as even the best systematic desensitisation approach only manages the situation. Callahan once said of these approaches and specifically CBT that we are "training the client to withstand and cope with a lot more misery than they ever thought they were capable of". None of these therapies actually remove the trauma.

So what alternatives do we have?
It is my belief the only hope we have of alleviating the suffering is to use psychosensory based therapies. EMDR has had some success, as does the more current process called Havening, which works directly on Amygdala-based disorders. Callahan Techniques TFT has a massive success rate in treating PTSD, so much so that in the Bosnian conflict the Chief Medical Officer put out an order that the primary treatment for PTSD must be TFT. My personal experience as a TFT practitioner and trainer is that the efficacy rate is excellent and for many years this was the 'go-to' technique for this condition and still to a huge degree is the base technique I use in sessions with my clients. The key about this intervention it is that it works independent of any belief system in it and also works content free, so the client does not have to reconnect to

the trauma and vocalise it to the therapist. This is good practice in my opinion.

I remember Richard Bandler, the co-creator of NLP once saying he was dealing with a rape victim who had been to counselling for a number of years and had been required by the counsellor to repeat the story of the incident over and over again, which she obviously found quite upsetting. Richard's question was "WHY . . .wasn't it bad enough the first time"?

In my opinion any therapy which requires you to re-traumatise yourself repeatedly is somewhat flawed in its approach, and bordering on cruel.

I believe we must look at techniques, which can operate content free, or with minimum recall access, to treat effectively. I also believe that speed is the key.

To use a metaphor; if picking up a trauma is like picking up a bag, how long did it take you to pick up the bag? So you may have carried the bag a long time, but how long would it take you to put the bag down? The answer is not 'slowly'.

Why the case for 'fast'?

We are electro-magnetic and electro-chemical beings and our neurology operates at the speed of light, which is 186,000 miles per second, which is fast.

So if a trauma can be encoded at the Amygdala-based level at that speed then why can it not be uncoded rapidly too?

In Psychosensory techniques we are finding faster ways to do this all the time.

My background as an engineer allows me to see issues maybe a little differently than traditional therapists.

I use a computer analogy to try to explain this. We are very much like computers, a whole bunch of systems designed to enable us to function and operate well. Such systems are digestive, respiratory, circulatory, psychological, lymphatic, optical, neurological and limbic. All these systems are trying to keep us in a natural state of homeostasis, our natural and optimal state.

Now if a trauma is installed into the limbic system this can transfer into other systems, such as the digestive system causing IBS or the respiratory system causing COPD or asthma. A bit like a virus on a computer stopping other programs from working effectively and slowing down the system.

An IT specialist would come along and remove the virus from the system allowing it to return to its optimal performance, well I propose we can do the same, and just as quickly with the right therapy, and these are the 'fast' therapies. Psy-Tap, Kinetic Shift, TFT.

I often draw a comparison here . . . I am not in IT (information technology) but more HT (human technology) and I am working with your 'neck-top' computer and returning it to its optimal performance state, which we call homeostasis.

Another simple analogy I draw is your trauma is like a DVD you keep watching over and over again and you have become an expert in the 'story', which remember is no longer happening. It happened and it is over, the only place it is being kept alive is in your right brain. So why do you watch the DVD over and over? The answer is you are still trying to find a way to escape from the initial encoding moment, and until you do you will keep activating it over and over again.

In psychology this is called as 'repetition compulsion'. A good example of repetition compulsion is when a woman who has been in an abusive or violent relationship enters into a series of these relationships. This is not because she enjoys the experience but she is trying to find an escape from the primary trauma and will keep entering the same experience and environment in search of that escape. This pattern is why current management therapies often do not work. Instead, the trauma needs to be disabled from operating, a little like removing the DVD from the player so you can no longer watch it. You cannot comment or react on what you are not experiencing, so if we can disable the ability to experience the trauma then it can no longer affect you. It is like trying to ask someone to tell you of a holiday they have not been on.

So we can uncode an encoded trauma. EMDR does this to some degree as does NLP Reframing. In my system Psy-Tap (Psychosensory Techniques and Principles) I posit that speed is the key. Also a good understanding of the process of trauma embedding and replaying is important. We then have to break the pattern, so it no longer gives us the outcomes we don't want to have.

In my system I view emotional states like the end result of an engineering process. What is required neurologically, biologically and biochemically to achieve the emotional state? The question then is, what is the earliest and best point to stop this pattern, this process from happening?

Let me use anger as a simple example. Currently the British Association of Anger Management is offering a 30-hour programme . . .30 hours!

I propose you can stop anger in one second.

First thought, what is the pattern? What is the process required to generate a state, such as anger, and what is required neuro-biologically to achieve this. Second thought, how can I interrupt this pattern and disable the ability to generate a less than useful emotion?

So, please try this. Think of something now that you can get angry about, scale it on one to 10 with 10 being furious and one being nothing but a memory. Now take the index and second finger of your right hand and push down on the little finger of your left hand (pushing it away from the third finger). Done? Good. Now while doing that try to get angry. And find you cannot.

Witchcraft? No, a simple function, when you do that with your hands you are unable to make a fist, if you are unable to make a fist the signal goes to the fight or flight response (in that basic Amygdala part of the brain) and turns it off. If it is rage, then do the same but also drop your jaw so it is loose, if you cannot clench your teeth you cannot do rage either.

This simple technique gives you immediate control over whether you wish to be angry or not. There are times where anger may be appropriate. This simple technique enables you to decide though. I believe you do not want to manage anger; you should be able to choose anger or not to have anger.

You are also doing something else. We know more now about neuro-plasticity, that is how our brains can change. By doing actions such as these we can fire off new neural pathways so you may react 'less often' with a default anger reaction as the old neural pathways get 'pruned' and new ones get established.

So what about Trauma?
Well, when the Amygdala fires off its Fight, Flight or Freeze response the sympathetic nervous system becomes activated, this includes the mouth becoming dry, an increase in heart rate, blood flowing to the muscles in preparation to fight or flee, and the pupils dilating to enable us to see as much as we can.

So looking at the last element, the pupils dilating, if we shine a light into the eyes the pupils will contract automatically. This creates a neurobiological conflict and shuts down the Amygdala response. We can then use a system called VCART Visual Coding and Repatterning Technique. Using simple cross hemispheric switching in conjunction with the light regulates the Amygdala and sympathetic nervous system response, which in turn collapses the trauma. We can also use a strobe light, then we are working faster than the Amygdala can react.

Clients say it is like someone has taken an 'eraser' and cleaned the whiteboard of the memory of the trauma. Actually what has happened is the memory is still there but it is stored appropriately. It can no longer be accessed as a working memory and thus cannot create the emotional response.

The brain now understands the trauma is no longer happening now and as such cannot react to it anymore. Even when you try to provoke the memory and ask the client to 'get it back' or to initiate the trauma, they are unable to.

All of this often takes just minutes.

Avoid A-Void
The final and very necessary element is to do what I call avoid a-void. Once the client is no longer able to access the negativity around the trauma they may try to replace it with other negative patterns, because that is familiar and easy.

The brain is not being lazy here, just efficient and will go to fill the space with an easy option. So to override this we need to 'fill in' the new space with positive and enabling thoughts, feelings and emotions. For this there are many techniques, I use a system called PIE or Positive Imagery Exercise. It goes like this.

Raise the right hand up and to the right of you so you are looking up at it. Look into your palm and create a compelling image of what you want to be.

Assume that nothing can fail.

Then double the intensity of the picture and brighten it.

Then double it again and again. When it looks amazing and

only then take a deep breath in and as you exhale pull the image into your chest and absorb it through your heart then as you breathe in intensify the image and as you exhale drive the feeling through your body into every cell, muscle, nerve, fibre and tissue until you are saturated with the good feeling. Then repeat with another good image.

Do this as often as you like . . . after all who can ever have enough good feelings? And they are much better than the bad feelings. Right?

I can be contacted at www.kevinlaye.co.uk

Get it Sorted 3: Dr Mark Chambers writes

NEURO-LINGUISTIC PROGRAMMING (NLP)

I think this man is suffering from memories
Sigmund Freud 1895

We all have memories and, if they are traumatic we can suffer from them. When Freud was writing, the treatment options for those suffering from memories were limited.

That has changed and now many diverse healing techniques have been found to help. One approach which has a good track record of success is Neuro-Linguistic Programming (NLP). NLP techniques have been applied effectively in people suffering as a consequence of psychological trauma, itself often occurring in the context of physical trauma.

NLP arose from the collaborative work of Richard Bandler and John Grinder in the 1970s. Though neither of them were therapists in the conventional sense (Bandler was a mathematician, Grinder a linguistics professor), they were set the challenge of modelling the excellence of three very successful professionals working in the psychological field: Fritz Perls, Milton Erickson, and Virginia Satir.

The English anthropologist Gregory Bateson, a colleague of John Grinder's at The University of California, presented this challenge. He asked them to see if they could identify "the difference that makes the difference." What was it that these people were doing that seemed to produce significantly better results than those being achieved by other therapists? In a collaboration that lasted for about six years, and with the assistance of many colleagues, they evolved a methodology for modelling this excellence which they called Neuro-Linguistic Programming (NLP).

This is essentially an approach to learning and techniques which are applicable in any endeavour where learning and change are occurring, including therapy. NLP techniques are now employed in, for example, education, business, the performing arts, sport and coaching, as well as the world of therapy.

What is NLP?
NLP is essentially an attitude, and angle of approach. From this it develops a creative curiosity about the structure of human experience that allows us to learn and change how we think, feel, behave and communicate. From this emerges a methodology (modelling) and hence a series of techniques.

NLP is all about freedom: freedom from the baggage of limiting beliefs.

Freedom in this context is the knowledge that nothing we believe is 'true'. By directing our focus and setting our direction, our beliefs determine our state, which is the single most important factor in generating our outcomes. A belief is nothing more than a feeling of certainty about a thought.

This is important. The body keeps the score: feelings are pre-linguistic, but they determine where we place our focus. In the process of change, we change how we feel by changing what we believe will happen in the future.

To break this down a little more: "neuro" refers to how our nervous system perceives and interprets information. "Linguistic" refers to how we communicate this interpretation to others and ourselves. "Programming," describes the patterns of thought, feeling and behaviour that stem from this interpretation. An appreciation of this model gives us many points of interaction to modulate and modify the processing and generate alternative and more desirable outcomes. In other words adaptation and change, a model of the learning process.

Learning to do what works
NLP is a learning technology, but it can have therapeutic benefits.

It presupposes that people are not broken and so do not need fixing. Much can be achieved by using this model. Key things are:
- placing the focus in the future and setting goals
- building rapport with self and others
- building motivation and determination
- accessing resources and taking appropriate action

In other words, doing something. If you decide to go for NLP you will be reflecting, learning to measure your feelings and achievements and becoming familiar with your senses and feelings. This means you can be constantly checking that you are on course, and if not, developing and applying new ways of processing to get back on course.

NLP and trauma

In the context of trauma, we will be looking at the response to intuitions and perceptions (the neuro bit), expressed cognitively and externally in language and behaviour (the linguistic and programming bit). Change any part and the results will change: a new programme. The application of the knowledge of NLP allows awareness of process to emerge. This, in turn, enables adaptation and change.

Concentrating on the 'now'

This approach does not require any exploration of the past for 'causes'. This is the province of psychotherapy. It was because this approach was not getting good results that Bateson set Bandler and Grinder off on their quest in the first place.

Instead, NLP acknowledges the essential function of the brain is to make things familiar. This is an instinct even more fundamental than survival. An NLP approach takes the position that the best thing about the past is that it is over. There is only now, and that in the now there is neurological processing taking place. If this processing is producing good results, this can be modelled and taught to others. If the results are not good, the active patterning can be identified and disrupted, so that the triggers for dysfunctional states can, in future, generate more desirable outcomes.

The two key factors to be identified are intention and patterning. The third principle then is utilisation. This means identification of your existing resources and directing them to where they can most usefully be deployed. We can add more resources if necessary. This is learning, not therapy. The modelling of success.

In practice, this model leads us to asking useful questions. The first question is how people are doing what they are doing? How are they doing their 'problem' state?

Once this is done we can look at people who have experienced trauma and found their way through the consequences successfully. How did they do it? This knowledge helps with accessing the resources and building the strategies for someone suffering with trauma to employ, so they can achieve their desired outcomes. This is an educational process of reflection, learning, transformation and evolution, with the focus in the future at all times.

Even before asking these questions the first task is to access and install hope, which comes from the belief that a positive outcome is possible. Once this hope and belief are in place, it is possible to negotiate what are the goals the person wants. Resources to get there can then be identified, many of which are already in place, just forgotten.

An NLP practitioner will ask you: "What are they already doing that is helping in any way?" This question stems from the principle that it is much easier to redirect a stream than to dam it up.

The next part is building motivation, determination and resolution by making the desired outcomes so compelling that nothing will stop them being achieved. This is called state change: once their state is right, people can then get on and do what needs to be done: take action.

To do this it is best to travel light and leave baggage behind. Build in some regular reflection so appropriate adjustments can be made and the pattern is complete.

Who gets traumatised and who doesn't
Many people who have been through potentially traumatic experiences seem to come through relatively unscathed. After a period of adjustment their equanimity appears restored. But about 25 percent of people who experience a traumatic event

do go on to experience significant and lasting effects. This seems to be influenced by both the severity of the trauma and their emotional state at the time. The more anxious they were, the more likely were ongoing problems. Highly-hypnotisable people appear more vulnerable. Post-Traumatic Stress Disorder is a recognised syndrome, but many people exhibit some but not all of the symptoms which it covers. These include intrusive symptoms, avoidance, more negative thoughts and moods and alterations in arousal and reactivity.

The symptoms have to have lasted more than a month, cause functional impairment and not be caused by something else (for example medication, substances or other illnesses). Symptoms may occur at any time after the trauma, possibly months later.

Intrusive memories or emotions are the most common after-effects of trauma. If you are suffering, often you can remember some aspects of the triggering event and this recall is distressing, even if incomplete. Also, you feel the distress in the present: as if it is happening now. The memory is not stored away in the past, but is psychologically active now.

Intrusive visual flashbacks and nightmares may occur. Emotional flashbacks are also common, with unpredictable irritability, emotional outbursts and ability and poor concentration. Anxiety, depression and obsessional patterns of thought and behaviour can develop, often with physical symptoms: such as excessive tiredness, headaches, aches and pains, gut disturbances, breathing problems and rashes. Hyper-vigilance, with hyper-arousal and poor sleep is common. Aggression, lack of trust, wariness, guardedness and suspicion are often evident, as are avoidance behaviours and emotional numbness, which can be severe, often with self-loathing and also with self-harm and self-destructive behaviours.

All this can lead to emotional withdrawal, with consequent

relationship problems, employment difficulties and family disintegration, as well as psychological problems including profound depression and substance abuse.

The effects of trauma stretch from the past, with the dysfunctional storage of memories, through the present with the protective and dissociative influence of defence mechanisms, through into the future with the disconnected parts of the personality conflicting and causing chaos for the individual. All these aspects can be addressed and helped using NLP techniques.

NLP techniques for trauma
Perhaps the most widely used NLP technique employed in the management of severe psychological trauma is Double Disassociation, or Visual-Kinaesthetic Disassociation. An NLP practitioner will help you to step back from your current experience and observe and learn from a dispassionate position, a "clean third". This in itself is often enough to help you process memories so they can be stored. In double disassociation a further step out of the observer position is taken, so you watch the watcher watching the traumatic experience, (with what is called 'shielding' to protect you while you process your experiences) Throughout all this, you will be anchored repeatedly in the present so your experiences can help you with real and present life.

Another frequently employed NLP technique is Six Step, or Parts Reframing. This is especially useful for integrating and unifying the various parts of your personality at play in the situation, both those parts accessible to conscious awareness and those parts which are working at an unconscious level and providing the defensive patterning which is in operation.

This process establishes contact between the unconscious

parts and the parts functioning of which you are aware. You can then begin establishing the common positive intentions all the parts have for you and finding ways forward which satisfy and unify all parts. There are various ways this can be done. All involve acknowledgement that there is a positive intention that underlies all emotion and behaviour at some level (often all the parts will be trying to protect you from the effects of the traumatic experience). The NLP practitioner will work to strengthen your ego and build your self-belief as well as helping you find beliefs and values which are better adapted to what you want from life. With these new resources in place you can make the changes you want.

The approaches and interventions of NLP have been developed and refined over nearly 50 years now in many diverse fields. They provide many learning tools which complement therapeutic approaches elegantly, being generally swift and straightforward to apply. Calibration and attention to detail is critical. Small, subtle nudges applied judiciously can rapidly generate significant results.

It is no longer necessary to suffer from memories.

I can be contacted at https://anlp.org/member/mark-chambers
Reference:
{1}Diagnostic and Statistical Manual of Mental Disorders (5th Edition)
American Psychiatric Association (2013)
Washington DC
www.dsm.psychiatryonline.org

Get it Sorted 4: Dr Sue Peacock writes

EYE MOVEMENT DESENSITISATION AND REPROCESSING (EMDR)

What is EMDR?

EMDR was developed by Dr Francine Shapiro who noticed that under certain situations, eye movements reduced the intensity of upsetting and disturbing thoughts. She continued to research this phenomenon and in 1989, she published her successful results of treating patients who had experienced trauma in the *Journal of Traumatic Studies*. Over time, EMDR has evolved and developed into a set of standardised protocols and various treatment approaches.

EMDR can sound a bit weird. To try to make sense of it, let's compare the emotional aspect to the more familiar physical aspects of health. For example, if you cut your hand, your body will work to heal the cut. However, if you have a foreign body in your hand or the cut is frequently irritated, the cut will become infected and painful. The foreign body can be considered to be a block to healing. And when you remove the foreign body, healing starts.

With EMDR a similar process is at work, but with our mental health processes. Usually the information processing part of the brain will instinctively move towards positive mental health. However, if this information processing system is blocked or unsettled by a traumatic or disturbing event, the 'emotional wound' gets worse and can cause a lot of distress. Using detailed EMDR protocols, we can remove the block and the natural healing process can start.

Interestingly, along with other psychotherapeutic approaches, no-one really knows how they work in the brain. We do know that if someone gets really upset, then that moment of the upsetting incident gets stuck in time and the brain is unable to process the information in its usual way. So remembering a trauma can feel as bad as when you first experienced the event – your feelings, the images, sounds and smells haven't changed because they haven't been processed.

Following a successful EMDR treatment, normal information processing in the brain restarts. When the traumatic event is brought to mind, you may remember the event but it is less upsetting and your feelings, the images, sights and sounds are less distressing. Research suggest that the process of EMDR is similar to what happens naturally in our REM sleep patterns or whilst we are dreaming.

To summarise, EMDR is a physiologically-based psychotherapy which helps people see a difficult life event or trauma in a different and less upsetting way.

Before you start
If you wish to consider using EMDR, please use someone who is qualified in the eight-phase approach put forward by Shapiro. This is the EMDR approach that has been scientifically researched.

Questions you might consider asking a practitioner prior to EMDR treatment:

1. Have they received training from an EMDR accredited training company?
2. Have they kept up to date with the latest protocols and developments?
3. How many cases have they treated with your particular issue?
4. What is their success rate?

What happens in EMDR treatment sessions?
The aim of this therapy is to completely process the experiences causing distress. By processing I don't mean just talking about it. In this context, processing means creating a learning state which allows your distressing experiences to be dealt with and stored appropriately within your brain. Therefore you will be able to learn what was useful from that experience and the brain will store it with appropriate emotions, which can help you in the future. Inappropriate beliefs, emotions, behaviours and sensations within your body will be discarded. The aim of EMDR treatment is to leave you with understanding, perspective and emotions that will lead to useful interactions and behaviours. It usually takes between three and seven sessions to make progress with each session lasting 60 to 90 minutes.

I want to tell you more about what happens in a course of EMDR sessions so here is a brief overview of the eight phase treatment protocol – a full description can be found in *Eye Movement Desensitisation and Reprocessing* by Francine Shapiro.

Phase 1: The clinician will take your history to get a complete picture, looking at negative thoughts and whether there are any long-standing patterns of unhelpful behaviour and the symptoms. They will also ask about your history of trauma and past and present triggers. Your future goals will be discussed, mutually decided and prioritised. The clinician would also be looking for what current available resources you have to deal with the issue(s). Other factors looked at in this phase are the current level of emotional disturbance, current emotional stability, social support and physical health. An EMDR professional will also ask about what medication you are taking, drug and alcohol use and explore any tendency you have to dissociate from the issue. In this session a rapport, an atmosphere of support and trust should be developed between the two of you.

Phase 2: At this stage the main focus is still preparation for EMDR treatment and it's very important to continue building the therapeutic relationship. It's really important that you feel safe, and able to speak openly and freely. The clinician will explain the theory of EMDR and put it into your personal context and talk to you about what you can expect from treatment sessions. In this phase the clinician will teach you a variety of relaxation techniques, so you can calm yourself during the emotional disturbance that may arise during or after a session. It is important you can take care of yourself.

Phases 3-6: This phase accesses each problem area for you, so it can be effectively processed using EMDR. It is important that you are aware that the only thing in our past is our memories. The clinician will identify the aspects of the target to be processed. You will then be asked to select a specific picture from the target event that best represents your memory. Next you will choose a statement that expresses a negative self-belief associated with the event which they focus on. Common statements are:

o "I could have died",
o "I'm useless/ helpless"
o "I'm in danger".

Then you will be asked to pick a positive self-statement you would rather believe such as:

- "I am alive"
- "I can succeed"
- "I'm in control"
- "I'm safe now".

The clinician will next ask you to estimate how true you feel (that is feel not think) your positive statement is on a scale of 1= completely false, 7=completely true. You will also be asked to identify negative feelings such as fear or anger and notice whether you have any physical sensations (things such as cold hands, tightness in stomach, tight shoulders). Next you will be asked to rate how disturbed you feel by the event using a scale called Subjective Units of Distress (SUDS) with 0=no disturbance to 10=the worst feeling you could possibly have.

You will then be instructed to focus on the picture, the negative thought and bodily sensations whilst engaging in EMDR processing. This uses a technique called bilateral stimulation which can be visual, tactile or auditory and works on a fixed left right pattern which helps you to process memories in a new way. This could be following the clinician's instructions and performing a certain set of eye movements or responding to a programme of taps from the clinician. This is not difficult or challenging and you will just be asked to notice whatever happens.

After each set of bilateral stimulation, the clinician will ask you to let your mind go blank and to notice whatever picture, thought, feeling, sensation or memory comes into your mind. The clinician will choose the next focus of attention depending upon what you say. These bilateral stimulation sets will be repeated until your distress levels (using the SUDS scale) are right down and you feel no distress in relation to the targeted memory. At this point, you will be asked to think of your positive self-statement and focus on it during the next set of distressing events.

Phase 7: This phase is closure. The clinician will remind you of the relaxation and self-calming activities taught in phase 2.

Phase 8: This phase looks at the progress you have made so far and ensures that all the incidents that caused distress have been processed effectively.

Does EMDR work?

The research suggests that EMDR for post-traumatic stress is an effective and efficient treatment. In the UK, back in 2005, the National Institute of Clinical Excellence acknowledged EMDR as an effective treatment for post-traumatic stress. The American Psychological Association included EMDR on their list of "Empirically Validated Treatments" for civilian post-traumatic stress. Also, the International Society for Traumatic Stress Studies, American Psychiatric Association, the World Health Organisation and the U.S. Department of Veterans Affairs and Department of Defence defined EMDR as an effective psychotherapy for post-traumatic stress.

The gold standard of research is 'randomised controlled trials' (RCTs) as they are most powerful method of ascertaining the effectiveness of procedures. Currently there are over 30 RCTs on EMDR and post-traumatic stress. Overwhelmingly, these RCTs demonstrate superiority for EMDR against its comparisons.

Benefits of EMDR:

According to the EMDR institute website, research has shown that between 84 and 100 percent of people with post-traumatic stress who had experienced one trauma recovered fully after three to six sessions. There have also been rapid results with combat veterans with three out of four recovering fully after 12 sessions.

- ○ It helps to reduce the anxiety and depression that people who experience post-traumatic stress often have.
- ○ It helps the person to re-establish a positive outlook for the future and to make emotional connections.
- ○ It helps people to recover from trauma without avoiding all the things they associate with the traumatic event, as often avoidance is a coping strategy in people with post-traumatic stress.
- ○ People who receive EMDR treatment often report valuable insight into their negative beliefs and the trauma they experienced.

Limitations of EMDR

EMDR like other therapies will require you to open up and confront painful memories, thoughts and feelings. Understandably this can temporarily make things seem worse before they start getting better, so sometimes you may feel more distressed than ever as you start confronting their past traumas.

After an EMDR session, some clients will continue to process trauma-related issues between sessions which can be distressing. This is why it is vital to have a variety of self-calming strategies.

I can be contacted at www.apaininthemind.co.uk/

No D in PTSD

Get it Sorted 5: Alan Freeburn writes

COGNITIVE BEHAVIOURAL THERAPY (CBT)

What is CBT?

Cognitive Behavioural Therapy, or CBT, is a talking therapy that can help you manage your problems by changing the way you think and behave.

It's based on the idea that our thoughts, emotions, physical sensations and behaviours are all connected and affect each other.

For example, if you have a negative thought such as, "If I leave the house today, I'll have a panic attack," it can lead to emotions such as anxiety and panic which then trigger physical sensations in the body such as rapid breathing, increased heart rate, churning stomach and many others. These emotions and sensations then influence behaviour, perhaps meaning that you avoid going out in order to protect yourself.

The next time you think about leaving the house this same vicious cycle can then be triggered again meaning you may stay in this pattern of thoughts, emotions and behaviour leading to longer term problems.

CBT is a process where you learn to manage thoughts and behaviours, learn new skills and focus on the future to help manage difficulties such as anxiety, depression and trauma. By shifting the focus from negative thoughts and worries, to taking action and challenging cognitions, you regain control of your mental wellbeing. Many clients find this process works well for them and as well as learning skills to manage their mental and physical health they also learn skills for life!

CBT can be used in several ways. It may be used in a group format, to help a larger number of people with a similar issue. Or there are ways where you can access CBT online, which means you can do 'self-help' when it's convenient.

Often though, it is delivered as a one-to-one course of treatment with a therapist. This normally takes the form of 45-60 minute sessions, weekly or fortnightly for six to 12 sessions. This can vary depending on the provider and the severity of the condition.

What it does
CBT mainly focuses on dealing with the current problem rather than looking to the past. Although initially, it is often important to look to the past to understand how and why the problems have developed.

CBT is often called a talking therapy, and so it is. The talking part is what happens during the sessions when you the client and a therapist meet. They might focus on issues, setting goals, learning techniques to challenge difficult thoughts and overcome challenging behaviours as well as other skills such as relaxation and assertiveness. However, most of the work is done *between* sessions with the client practising the new skills: getting out of their comfort zone, challenging their thoughts and learning to control physical sensations.

What happens in CBT sessions

One of the starting points is an assessment to get a thorough understanding of the problem as well as how it developed. This sometimes means finding out what has happened to you throughout your life. If you opt for this type of therapy, the therapist will work with you in developing this shared understanding. (in CBT this is called 'the formulation'). It may be that events from childhood, for example, make you more vulnerable to later problems – if your childhood was disrupted in some way or you didn't have the opportunity to develop strong relationships or coping skills. Further adverse events in life may reinforce this over a period of time.

However, people can often cope with these things in life, finding ways to get by, perhaps for years. Then a build-up of stress or a particular incident can trigger an overwhelming amount of anxiety or a panic attack. This may lead to a change of behaviour such as avoidance of the difficult circumstances which feels more comfortable in the short-term, but leads to problems over a longer period of time. We become stuck.

CBT and PTSD

CBT is used for a variety of anxiety conditions including trauma or Post Traumatic Stress Disorder. The NICE* Guidelines for the management of PTSD states that: "All PTSD sufferers should be offered a course of trauma-focused psychological treatment (trauma-focused cognitive behavioural therapy or eye movement desensitisation and reprocessing)." As the name suggests, the main aim within this CBT treatment is to focus on the trauma. This is usually done after several sessions to help you to develop skills to get basic emotional stability and develop a good therapeutic relationship with your therapist before moving on to the more challenging trauma work. In that part, like CBT generally, we look at challenging thoughts and assumptions, as well as behaviours. That might include undertaking graded exposure work in a real-life situation (this is called *in vivo* exposure), such as building up to revisiting the scene of a trauma incident, over a period of time.

In addition there is strong evidence for the use of imaginal exposure. This can require guiding you through a process of recalling the incident in detail over several sessions to allow the proper processing of the memories of the incident. This can help reduce disturbing symptoms. Then time can be spent trying to orient you back onto your previous lifestyle, re-engaging with previous pastimes, hobbies and activities and helping you set goals for the future.

How it works: The 'CBT' of it
I have already mentioned the vicious cycle and how thoughts, feelings, physical symptoms and emotions all influence each other. The key to treatment is a focus on changing elements within that cycle to make it a more positive one. We can't change emotions directly, but we can change thoughts and behaviours.

Cognitive
The cognitive part is all about how we think about things, events, situations and symptoms as well as the beliefs we have about ourselves and others. In therapy, we look at those thoughts, try to reason with them or challenge them with evidence to the contrary; perhaps looking at things from a different point of view.

If we take the idea that how we think affects how we feel, then when we challenge and change thoughts we can change the emotions that the thoughts are creating. This might take the form of a thought diary where we try and capture negative automatic thoughts and begin to challenge them. One of the main ideas behind CBT is that we have these cognitive distortions, or thinking errors, which keep us trapped in this destructive way of thinking which maintains our difficulties. By paying attention to these thoughts and recognising the errors we can then learn to challenge them which can lead to a better understanding and influence how we feel.

Behaviour
Changing our behaviours can have several different uses. It can help manage symptoms by teaching you how to relax or simply as a short-term distraction from the symptoms. Behaviour change can also be used to challenge beliefs and automatic thoughts. This takes the form of behavioural experiments, testing out the assumptions and automatic thoughts in practice.

In other words this means putting yourself in a place where you can experience anxiety, then resisting the temptation to escape and realising that the assumptions may be wrong. In this way we can adapt our thinking, reframe our assumptions and learn to approach situations differently.

We can also use exposure. The body gets used to experiencing and dealing with the anxiety through this process of exposure. By staying in the situation, the symptoms reduce. By repeating this over a period of time for the same situation the body adjusts and stops releasing adrenaline which again reduces the physical symptoms. You can then repeat this with increasingly difficult situations until you are able to manage a broad range of situation previously avoided. In other words, we get used to the situation and the body does not react as if threatened – as we practise this in different situations we regain more control over our lives.

The behavioural experiments are tested out between sessions. This is the 'homework' part of CBT. Testing out theories and assumptions, gaining new knowledge, learning new skills and then discussing this in session with the therapist.

Over a period of time, you can learn to adjust and manage thoughts, change and adapt behaviour and learn skills such as relaxation, problem-solving and many others. In this way you develop the skills to better cope with your circumstances, understand your condition and improve your mental health.

Therapy
One factor that helps the effectiveness of CBT, and any therapy for that matter, is having a good therapeutic relationship. In other words the therapist tries hard to create a relaxed and useful space in which the client can feel safe enough to explore their difficulties and work toward resolution.

At times it's important that the therapist challenges you – the client – to confront negative thoughts and assumptions or support you to do things that are difficult. If not, then we as therapists can end up overprotecting you, the client which means that you are not learning the skills required to manage your difficulties. This can result in clients becoming dependent on therapists and that's definitely not what CBT is about!

Does it work? The evidence
NICE guidelines recommend the use of CBT for depression, Obsessive Compulsive Disorder and anxiety conditions including panic and post traumatic stress. There's also good evidence for using it in treating anger, sleep difficulties, chronic pain and chronic fatigue. CBT can be used on its own but it is often used in conjunction with medication.

There are a wide variety of techniques within CBT. One of the strongest supported is exposure. This is basically putting yourself in a situation that you would normally avoid, experience the anxiety rather than escape, and then leave the situation when calmer.

It may be you have a fear of spiders, for example. We would then use CBT to help you overcome this fear a little bit at a time by getting used to thoughts about spiders or practising getting used to images of a spider, for example, in a gradual way before moving on to more challenging steps until you eventually reach your goal.

I can be contacted at info@tfltherapies.com

References
*NICE - National Institute for Health and Care Excellence. The NHS follows their guidelines for treatment)
(ref: www.nice.org.uk/guidance/cg26)
www.nhs.uk/conditions/cognitive-behavioural-therapy/Pages/Introduction.aspx#prosandcons)

No D in PTSD

Get it sorted 6 : Liz Sharpe writes

COUNSELLING, AND OTHER THERAPIES

What it is: person-centred therapy

Post traumatic stress affects the whole of the person – it can't be locked away in a box and confined to just one part or timeline of life. Instead, it is like ripples in a pond, it potentially impacts on relationships with family and friends, work and study, hobbies and interests and physical and emotional health. It can lead to addiction and impact on choices made in life and plans for the future.

One way of treating it is person-centred therapy. This was introduced to Britain in the late 1960s by Carl Rogers. It focuses on the principle of the 'here and now'. The therapist/counsellor will encourage you to explore and create positive change for yourself and think in the present, while looking at all those parts of life. Rogers believed that the client needed to learn to rely less on the judgements of others and instead turn inward to themselves for what to do. He said: "The client knows what hurts, what direction to go, what problems are crucial, what experiences have been deeply buried." (Rogers 1979)

The goal of therapy is to help you become more self aware and to be in control of creating positive change in your life. You will generally work 1:1 with your counsellor in 50-minute sessions. You have to want to be there in the session! It is a joint commitment between you and your therapist and the therapeutic relationship of trust that will help you get to where you want to be.

What will a person-centred counsellor believe about you as a person?

1. You are the expert in your own life.

2. A person will always develop or 'self actualise' and move towards his or her full potential – but this can get blocked by life experiences. The counsellor can help you to explore and use your own strengths and identity to get through those blocks.

3. Your counsellor will have undertaken extensive therapy on themselves so will know how it feels to be in the client's chair – it also means that he or she can be with you on your journey, without bringing their 'stuff' into the session.

4. If the counsellor provides a space and a therapeutic relationship that is congruent, empathic, and with unconditional positive regard – then you will move towards positive growth. (See just below for more explanation of these terms).

What are Congruence, Empathy and Unconditional Positive Regard?

These are the core conditions for person-centred counselling. Not everybody is fortunate enough to experience positive healthy relationships with people who are able genuinely to listen and share that space or story. What the counsellor will aim at is a feeling of having someone who is congruent – genuinely there to share your journey through confusion and distress. They will have security in themselves (a strong sense of their own core identity), this is necessary to be able to be with you and empathise with you in your world.

A counsellor can share that journey with you, through empathic understanding – so you, as a client, feel safe in the knowledge that the counsellor can hold that safe space for you to explore distressing or troubling feelings and memories. In successful counselling you experience the therapist as being someone who holds you in 'unconditional positive regard', that is they will be non-judgemental and value you as a person despite the pain and suffering you are sharing

Just imagine what can be achieved. . .

Other person-centred therapies include :
- ○ Gestalt
- ○ Human Givens
- ○ Transactional Analysis
- ○ Solution-focused brief therapy

Pyschodynamic therapy

Sigmund Freud was one of the early pioneers of psychodynamic therapy, but these days he often comes in for a lot of criticism within the modern therapy world. Freudian therapists would help people recognise recurring patterns of behaviour, and review early life experiences, emotions, thoughts, and beliefs to understand present-day problems. The goal of therapy is to help you to understand how the past is affecting your present life, and to gain self-awareness in your relationships with those around you. Sessions are normally over a longer period than person-centred therapy.

What does the psychodynamic therapist believe?
1. The therapist is the expert.
2. Our behaviours and feelings are rooted in unconscious motives, and our childhood experiences. Behaviour is determined – even slips of the tongue are due to the unconscious mind.
3. We are motivated by two instinctual drives – Eros (sex drive, and life instinct) and Thanatos (aggression and death instinct). Personality is shaped during stages of childhood.
4. The unconscious mind will store all of the upsetting feelings, urges and thoughts which are too painful for the client to consider. Those thoughts and feelings can still influence our behaviour. Psychodynamic therapy wants to bring about changes to that behaviour.
5. The therapeutic relationship between the client and therapist is key to exploring the relationship that the client has with people in his or her life. By looking closely at interpersonal relationships, the client can see his part in relationship patterns and be empowered to change that dynamic.

How would PTSD be tackled using a psychodynamic approach?
The therapist will focus on a number of different areas that may impact on symptoms of post traumatic stress – early childhood experiences and relationship and attachment to parents, current relationships and the defence mechanisms that you have in place (how you might be protecting yourself from the thoughts, feelings and triggers to the event).

Through the sessions, you will be guided to get in touch with and work through those painful unconscious feelings. For example, if you were expressing intense anger towards family for no apparent reason, this might be displaced feelings from the anger or blame you feel towards yourself. The therapist would explore this defence mechanism with you and support you towards dealing with situations in a healthier manner.

Other approaches within Psychodynamic therapies
- Jungian
- Psychoanalytic
- Kleinian
- Psychotherapy

All therapies - What happens in a first session?
The first session is usually information sharing and gathering, setting up the counselling agreement on number of sessions, confidentiality and boundaries, plus practicalities of when and where the sessions will take place. The counsellor will ask you questions about you and your life – your personal situation, symptoms that you are experiencing and what brought you to the point of booking a session. Following a traumatic event, it is possible that your symptoms include:
- Anger or irritability
- Isolation
- Substance abuse
- Sleep disturbances
- Hyper-vigilance
- Depression or anxiety
- Reckless behaviours

Talk to your counsellor about what you are experiencing. Therapy is a two-way effort – you need to be able to share as much information as you feel comfortable with. Therapy isn't a quick fix, but a journey of getting to know yourself and what you need to stay well.

All therapies - How could life be for you after the session(s)
- You will have a better understanding of yourself and be

able to feel confident to express your thoughts and feelings to others
- You will have healthier relationships with those around you
- You will have lost any feelings of guilt, insecurity and defensiveness
- You will have developed coping mechanisms for future situations
- You will have a clearer understanding of your own identity – your own judgements, meaning and experiences.
- By connecting with your inner self – you will feel increased self esteem, and overcome the reasons that brought you into therapy initially – the feelings of depression and anxiety, and behaviours that are likely to be as a result of feeling in distress (addiction, eating disorders, anger)

My approach
I am trained in a number of approaches including person-centred counselling.

If a client presented with post traumatic stress, my preference is to use other therapies such as Psy-TaP (which its founder Kevin Laye describes elsewhere in this book) alongside my counselling approach.

I have seen how a person can resolve very difficult experiences and issues using quick and effective tools such as these, without the need to explore deep painful memories. Counselling isn't necessarily the quickest method for dealing with symptoms such as flashbacks, and hyper-vigilance. However, the role of counselling within any therapy room is vital in my opinion and I would look for a therapist who has a counselling training background.

However, it should be recognised that there are also many clients who don't want a 'quick fix' and that needs to be respected. As a client, you may seek to understand what you have experienced to cause the initial or ongoing trauma, alongside a need to explore strategies for living your life now.

Person-centred counselling provides a solid framework in which to put meaning into your experiences, and develop the skills and qualities to move on with your life. Whatever form of support you opt for, the main thing is to find a therapist that you can feel rapport and form an alliance with. The success of therapy can be swayed by how comfortable you are in that therapy room, and willing to be part of that therapeutic alliance.

I can be contacted at www.liveyourlifetherapies.com

No D in PTSD

Index

Index

Index

Final words

GET IT SORTED. COME SEE ME NOW

I help people from all over the world using online services like Skype. Or you can come to see me face to face. If you want help face to face but live too far to come and see me get in contact and I will try to put you in touch with one of the therapists I have trained in techniques to help with PTSD.

No-one needs to live with PTSD, so get it sorted NOW!

I'm at

www.karlsmithhypnotherapy.com

AND there is more . . .

Heather Crawford and Nigel Meakin on Energy and Spiritual Work with PTSD

For more details: go to https://ukhypnosisacademy.com/ptsdbook

11357535R00062

Printed in Great Britain
by Amazon